Eat Your Colors

Green Food Fun

by Lisa Bullard

Capstone press

Mankato, Minnesota

A+ Books are published by Capstone Press,
151 Good Counsel Drive, P.O. Box 669, Mankato, Minnesota 56002.
www.capstonepress.com

1 2 3 4 5 6 11 10 09 08 07 06

Library of Congress Cataloging-in-Publication Data
Bullard, Lisa.
Green food fun / by Lisa Bullard.
      p. cm.—(A+ books. Eat your colors.)
      Includes bibliographical references and index.
      ISBN-13: 978-0-7368-5381-1 (hardcover)
      ISBN-10: 0-7368-5381-2 (hardcover)
      1. Food—Juvenile literature. 2. Green—Juvenile literature. I. Title. II. Series.
TX355.B924 2006
641.3—dc22   2005026670

Summary: Brief text and colorful photos describe common foods that are the color green.

Credits

Donald Lemke, editor; Kia Adams, designer; Kelly Garvin, photo researcher

Photo Credits

Capstone Press/Karon Dubke, all

Note to Parents, Teachers, and Librarians

This Eat Your Colors book uses full-color photographs and a nonfiction format to introduce children to the color green. *Green Food Fun* is designed to be read aloud to a pre-reader or to be read independently by an early reader. Photographs help listeners and early readers understand the text and concepts discussed. The book encourages further learning by including the following sections: Recipe, Glossary, Read More, Internet Sites, and Index. Early readers may need assistance using these features.

Table of Contents

Gobble Up Green

Fruity, crunchy, sweet, and healthy. Green foods are always a terrific treat. What is your favorite green food?

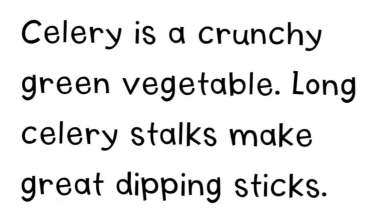

Celery is a crunchy
green vegetable. Long
celery stalks make
great dipping sticks.

6

8

Pack some pickles into a sandwich. These green veggies can be sweet, sour, or spicy.

Fruity Greens

Green grapes grow in groups called bunches. Pluck one off for a burst of sweet juice.

Inside a kiwifruit hides a sweet green treat. The tiny seeds are safe to eat and fun to crunch.

Do you eat honeydew?
These melons are as
big as bowling balls.
Each slice makes a
tasty green snack.

Avocados are green fruits.
Grow your own avocado
plant from the big round
seed inside.

Sweet Green Treats

Mint ice cream is frosty and green. Its cool burst of flavor comes from peppermint leaves.

Sweet lime gelatin
wiggles and jiggles.
This green snack has
a fresh citrus flavor.

Green Veggies

Green peas come in
their own tasty packages.
These tiny green veggies
grow together in pods.

Green bell peppers aren't always green. Let them grow a bit longer, and their shiny skin turns red.

Broccoli is a healthy green vegetable. It's just one of many fun green foods for you to explore.

Celery Sailing Ships

You can sail away on celery stalks and chomp into them for a healthy snack.

What You Will Need

2-3 stalks of celery

choice of fillings

choice of toppings

2-3 toothpicks

How to Make a Celery Sailing Ship

1. Clean the stalks of celery.

2. Have a grown-up cut the celery stalks into 3-inch (8-centimeter) pieces.

3. Take the leafy part from the top of the celery stalk. Stick a toothpick into the bottom of this piece. Only one point of the toothpick should be sticking out. Set aside.

4. Fill each piece of celery with cream cheese, peanut butter, or cheese spread. These are your ships.

5. Add raisins or sunflower seeds to the top of the spread. These are the passengers on your ships.

6. Pick up your leafy celery top. Stick the toothpick point down into the celery ship. Your ship now has a sail.

7. Throw fish-shaped crackers into the sea around your ship.

8. Eat and enjoy!

Glossary

citrus (SIT-ruhss)—an acidic, juicy fruit

gelatin (JEL-uh-tuhn)—a clear substance used in making jelly, desserts, and glue

peppermint (PEP-ur-mint)—a kind of mint plant; the oil from peppermint leaves is used to flavor foods.

pod (PAWD)—a long case that holds the seeds of certain plants, such as peas

vegetable (VEJ-tuh-buhl)—a plant grown to be used as food

Read More

Schuette, Sarah L. *Green.* Colors. Mankato, Minn.: Capstone Press, 2003.

Whitehouse, Patricia. *Green Foods.* The Colors We Eat. Chicago: Heinemann, 2002.

Internet Sites

FactHound offers a safe, fun way to find Internet sites related to this book. All of the sites on FactHound have been researched by our staff.

Here's how:

1. Visit *www.facthound.com*

2. Type in this special code 0736853812 for age-appropriate sites. Or enter a search word related to this book for a more general search.

3. Click on the Fetch It button.

FactHound will fetch the best sites for you!

Index